Great Value

LIFE LESSONS FROM A MONTANA COWBOY

Eldon Toews

Compiled by Janet Toews Berg
Cover Painting by Charlotte Sloan

WESTBOW
PRESS
A DIVISION OF THOMAS NELSON

WestBow Press books may be ordered through booksellers or by contacting:

WestBow Press
A Division of Thomas Nelson
1663 Liberty Drive
Bloomington, IN 47403
www.westbowpress.com
1-(866) 928-1240

ISBN: 978-1-4497-6691-7 (sc)
ISBN: 978-1-4497-6693-1 (hc)
ISBN: 978-1-4497-6692-4 (e)

Library of Congress Control Number: 2012917254

Printed in the United States of America

WestBow Press rev. date: 11/21/2012

Foreword

MANY TIMES, JESUS USED allegories to show us the great value of people. In Biblical times, an ox or ass was like a person's tractor or car and was needed for everyday living. Without one or both of these, life became much harder for the average person. So Jesus showed us that He values us and that when we fall into difficulties in life, He is ready to help us out because He values and loves us. This book is a collection of personal experiences with livestock that is intended to help you see how valuable you are to God.

"And He answered them saying, 'which of you shall have an ass or ox fall into a pit and will not immediately pull him out on the Sabbath Day?'" (Luke 14:5).

Great Value

It was 3:00 a.m., and I was exhausted, hungry, wet, and cold. But after a ten-minute break to change out of my snow-soaked pants and look for a dry pair of gloves, I was ready to head back out. It was snowing again, and the temperature was hovering around zero. I was working as a night calver. Already that night I'd carried four newborn calves into the calving shed and coaxed their reluctant two-year-old heifer mothers into pens with them. I helped each pair "mother up," seeing to it that each calf was beginning to nurse before checking on the next pair.

I knew I could not take much of a break, because I had seen two other heifers ready to give birth imminently. Calving season is the most exhausting, yet exciting, time of the year. A night calver is a cowboy who has such value for newborn calves that he is willing to forego sleep, regular meals, and comfort to spend long hours giving every calf a fighting chance to live. He knows that the combination of subzero weather and first-time mothers can be deadly. A calf can be born perfectly healthy, but unless the mother aggressively licks her baby dry to get the circulation going, it can die within minutes. Some two-year-old heifers don't do that because of their own fatigue, cold, or inexperience. The cowboy knows that if there is someone there to help, most calves can be saved.

All of us possess something of tremendous value—our souls. We have been given the ability to choose whether we keep and nurture that possession or overlook its value and squander it. It is easy in the busyness of life to ignore the value of our souls and give our attention to other temporal things that add to physical comfort and satisfaction.

Jesus Christ made an amazing statement: "What shall it profit a man if he gain the whole world but lose his own soul?" (Mark 8:36). From this we see that if we gain tremendous wealth but unwisely ignore our spiritual lives, we risk great loss in the end. Let us value our souls as much as a night calver values the lives of newborn calves. This can only happen if we trust in Jesus Christ, who has made provision for this through His life, death, and resurrection. Pursue a relationship with Him today.

The Round Pen

THE YOUNG, WILD COLT was terrified. His eyes were bulging, his breath came in snorts, and flecks of sweat dotted his glossy coat as he frantically circled the corral. His head was facing the outside, his rear turned toward the human standing motionless in the middle of the round pen.

Most young horses begin their lives out in open pasture or rangeland. At the owners' discretion they are brought in from the pasture to begin the breaking process with a skilled horsehand that knows how to turn a wild colt into a usable ranch horse.

This process starts in the round pen, which is a circular corral that the trainer puts the young colt in alone. The unbroken horse in the round pen is terrified because he realizes he is in the presence of someone more powerful than himself and freedom as he's known it before is gone. What the horse doesn't know is that endless possibilities await him—things and places that will become accessible to him when he learns to trust this two-legged human. He doesn't realize that what he sees as "freedom" could land him in a "loose horse sale" and possibly even in a glue factory.

Gradually the colt slows down and turns to face this leather-clad creature with the persistent and steady voice. When the colt's full attention is gained and he is no longer looking for ways to escape, the gentling process can begin. No horse can be gentled and become useable until he learns to submit to the trainer.

We, as people, have a Creator who sees a destiny in us and waits for us to slow down in our running and trying to get away from Him. Why would we want to escape His gentle voice and invitation to yield? Are we unaware of who He is and His intentions for us

and how good they are? Are we missing the stark reality that when we ignore Him and His plans and desires for us, we may end up in a "loose horse sale" and eventually in a "spiritual glue factory"? His plans for us are so much greater than we can imagine. The choice we have is to submit to His hand and let Him come close to us and take us into new expanses, territory we've not seen before—the best life we can possibly experience! What stands in the way of you and me saying to Him, "Okay, Lord, I want to submit to your plans for me. Help me overcome my fears and listen to Your words, stop running, and yield to You. I realize that it is best to have You in my life. Forgive me for resisting You. Thank you, Jesus, for dying on the cross to purchase me and give me a brand-new life. Help me today and each day to learn to submit to You and to what is good."

"'For I know the thoughts I think toward you' says the Lord, 'thoughts of peace and not of evil … to give you a future and a hope'" (Jeremiah 29:11)

"You are not your own, for you have been bought with a price, therefore glorify God in your body and in your spirit, which are God's" (1 Corinthians 6:19–20).

Shelter

It HAD BEEN A cold, miserable spring morning, but at last I had closed the gate on seventeen first-calf heifers that I had expected to calve that day or before the next morning. It was good to have a spacious barn that would give shelter from the biting cold wind that would lower the body temperature of a newborn calf so fast that its prospects of a future and life itself would drop dramatically.

Sure, those heifers had to get through the births of their calves, preferably without any problems, but the prospects of the births happening inside a good barn helped. Shelter from the wind and possible snow raised my hopes of a good calving night. Many Montana cattlemen use trees, windbreak, or hillsides for shelter from the weather to lower the number of calf losses due to the weather, but the blessings of a good barn are worth a lot.

In our pilgrimage, no one is guaranteed a peaceful, storm-free existence. In fact, Jesus said that "in this world you will have tribulation but be of good cheer for I have overcome the world" (John 16:33). If you are in the middle of a storm today, whether it's a relationship crisis, a health problem, or a financial difficulty, Jesus Christ invites us to take shelter in His love and care today. His Spiritual protection is invaluable.

"For You have been a shelter for me and a strong tower from the enemy" (Psalm 61:3).

Helper

ONE DAY WHEN I headed out the door to do my evening chores, my three-year-old son called after me. "Where are you going, Daddy?"

"Gotta feed those calves again," I told the inquisitive little boy.

"Quentin help?" was the quick reply, as the tousled-haired fellow scurried to get his chubby little legs into step with his lanky, sunburned young father.

The buckets of grain were heavy, but the toddler called loudly until I slowed down enough to let a dirty little hand grab the base of the bucket handle. He, of course, had no idea I was holding him up as his feet moved with the bucket to the troughs. When a neighbor stepped through the corral gate, he was quickly greeted with a smile and a cheery "Quentin helping Daddy."

Those words were no sooner spoken than the three-year-old stumbled and fell, his soft fingers becoming wedged between the bucket and its handle. As soon as I heard my son's cry of pain, I quickly set the buckets down and picked him up, wiping the tears away. The boy was soon laughing with pleasure and walking with pride again with his hand holding the bucket handle, "helping Daddy." He was too young to realize that the only assistance he was giving to his father was the pleasure of his company. The little toddler's dragging feet hardly slowed the big feet that had walked many miles, stood in the wind, carried feed in the mud and straw, walked on ice, and mounted unpredictable, saucy saddle horses. Hanging on was the little boy's only task.

As children of a heavenly Father, we too need help in getting around in life.

The "work" we do for God is more His letting us be with Him than our helping Him.

David had the right idea when he wrote, "Your right hand has held me up. Your gentleness has made me great. You enlarged my path under me, so that my feet did not slip" (Psalm 18:35–36). God takes our hands in His. He lifts us up gently. He holds us up. He lets us do things that look important, and though we often cannot see His strong hand on them, He is leading us on a smooth path, keeping us from blundering off into the wilderness. Will we still stumble and lose our balance on the path at times? Yes, but Scripture assures us that if we're clinging to His hand, our stumbling will not result in devastating falls. "The steps of a good man are established by the Lord, and He delights in his way. When he falls, he will not be hurled headlong because the LORD is the One who holds his hand" (Psalm 37:23–24 NASB).

Twin

SHE WAS ONLY A few days old, and already the little heifer calf was facing problems that could kill her. Her mother was a typical cow in the herd, known to always stay in the fence. She had had several calves and was a good enough mother, but her supply of milk was marginal. It took a strong, aggressive calf to get adequate milk from her. This spring she had had twins, and the smaller one was losing the competition.

Some cattlemen love twins because it increases the calving percentage, but others see it as more work. In this case, it was more work. I knew immediately when I spotted the heifer calf that she was not getting adequate nutrition. My compassion kicked in, and I decided drastic measures were called for if the calf were to have a chance.

I corralled a big-boned, brockle-faced cow who had lost her calf just two days before, and I set the calf to her. But after a few minutes the little heifer gave up; it was too stressful to have a strange cow kick her in the face every time she attempted to get something to eat.

Next I put the cow into the head catch and carefully made a rear-leg hobble out of about thirty lengths of baler twine. With a little encouragement, the runty twin was able to get a good meal. The pair were then turned out into a pen for the brockle-face to live with her twelve-inch hobble. I knew that the limitation to the mother (which might stay on for a week or a month) would be an advantage to the baby. Suddenly the twin had a future, thanks to a clever human and some throwaway baler twine put in the right place.

Jesus, who used mud to heal a blind man (in John 9:6), offers to take unusable things in our lives to bring us a future that we could never imagine. These things could include a negative past, fear of people, or situations that kick us in the face so often they seem unchangeable. Jesus offers us power today; ask him for help.

"..and the power of the Lord was with him to heal" (Luke 5:17).

Bucked Off

As THE GRAY GELDING disappeared over the ridge, I found myself on the ground in the snow. I considered myself to be a rough-string cowboy, but I had just been bucked off my horse.

Should I laugh or cry? Should I feel angry or frustrated? I limped through the snowy grass to retrieve my boot lying some distance away. I shook the snow out of it, brushed the snow off my stocking foot, and pulled it back on. I tried to remember what had happened, why I had been taken by surprise by the horse blowing up like that. I momentarily glared at the jagged rock I had missed by inches when I landed. Suddenly my mind was flooded with gratitude as I imagined what could have happened. I could have hit that rock in my fall, or if my boot had not come off, I could have been dragged for yards behind that horse with my head bouncing over rocks. Walking home with bruises and cold feet, I had plenty of time to think about what could have happened. It could have been worse.

Friend, this applies to our spiritual lives. When we stumble and fall, we momentarily feel loss at having been defeated and outdone by something bigger and more powerful than ourselves. We often feel regret and even anger. Yet in Christ we are more than conquerors; we cannot lose with His forgiveness and help. We need to remember to look beyond the daily ups and downs of life; spiritual happenings can be more important than physical occurrences.

"No, in all these things we are more than conquerors through Him [Christ] that loved us" (Romans 8:37).

The Gift

WHEN I UNWRAPPED THAT Christmas gift and saw it was cowboy boots, I was filled with an indescribable joy. As a boy, I had asked my parents for boots for several years and had not gotten them, so I was halfway prepared for disappointment. But there they were. When I slipped them on, they fit; it seemed they had been made just for me!

My feelings were partially composed of gratefulness to my parents for giving me this gift, which showed their understanding of my desires and identity. But also, wearing the boots, I had a confidence I had not experienced before; I felt that from now on, life could take any turn it may and I would be able to face it.

Sadly, six months from that Christmas Day, I could not drum up those same feelings. They were gone. So it is with the greatest thrill of objects, accomplishments, and relationships in this world when we try to make them fill a God-shaped vacuum inside our spirits. The Christ child of Bethlehem was born to fill the emptiness of mankind, caused by a broken relationship with God Himself. We must recognize that sin has separated us from a loving God and that we can only come into relationship with Him again with Jesus Christ. This is why He is called the "Greatest Gift."

I still wear boots, but they're on my feet, where they are meant to be, and not in my heart. This Christmas, with a believing heart, receive the greatest gift—Jesus Christ.

Fence Respect

Observe to do all the words of this law...
because it is your life.
—Deut. 32:46-47

IT WAS LATE WINTER, and I was riding toward the old, abandoned homestead when my horse "rolled his marbles", a long steady snort—an ominous sign of his distaste for something up ahead.

I had gone out almost every day that fall, combing the hills for fourteen missing cows. I had asked neighbors to be on the lookout, but there seemed to be no clues regarding their mysterious disappearance. Months passed, and then one day a neighbor casually mentioned the abandoned homestead. I had ridden past the homestead dozens of times, but it was fenced off so I did not approach it. I did not see the break in the fence behind the farmhouse. This time I opened the gate and went on to the yard. Everything about the barn and the old paint-peeled house appeared abandoned, but as I rode around the back of the house, my horse grew more and more reluctant.

I dismounted and entered what appeared to be a shallow root cellar, and there I pieced together a gruesome story: During a cold, windy, snowy day late in the fall, the missing cattle had probably broken through the fence and crowded on the east side of the abandoned farm home to avoid the wind. Somehow, likely because of their weight, the nearly horizontal door to a shallow root cellar gave way and a cow found herself in a warm, sheltered basement. The others must have followed her because it was warm inside. Then, during their milling around among old furniture and human keepsakes, the door to the outside was jammed shut. What had started out as a shelter became a prison, and they starved to death.

Although I was a cowboy accustomed to the ways of life and death, I found myself nauseated at the sight, and then angry and sad at the same time. "You idiots!" I shouted. "I rode by here within a hundred yards, but I didn't know you were stuck in here. Can't you old gals respect a fence? You would have been safe on the other side. I would have found you and brought you home to real shelter."

Jesus Christ promises life to all who obey Him. Staying within the parameters of His will is not always easy when something offers immediate comfort. It is important to remember that the temptation to step beyond His commands may be actually risky to our spiritual life and can end in devastating consequences. Take a spiritual warning today, partner, and obey Him.

Catch the Wind

"THAT DECREPIT THING LOOKS like it's been here forever," the cowboy commented to himself as he looked at the windmill. After two hours of riding the ridges, checking on cattle, he had ended up on the back side of the pasture, facing the windmill. Not ready to dismount his horse just yet, he allowed his thoughts to wander. He remembered the words of his foreman that morning: "Don't forget to grease that windmill on the east section of the arrowhead pasture. I don't think it's been serviced all summer." He mused about how somebody, years ago, went to a lot of work to erect the windmill to catch and harness the power of the wind to pump much-needed water for thirsty livestock. He also knew that for any machine to work well, it needed maintenance; a lack of grease would make the working parts dry, squeaky, and sluggish in catching the wind.

He roused himself and dismounted, pulling the grease gun from the saddlebag, where he had stuffed it after wrapping it in a rag early that morning. Carefully, he climbed the windmill to grease it and check the oil level in the gearbox.

Back on his tall bay gelding and heading for home, he felt a sense of satisfaction. He realized that part of his job to care for livestock was to keep this windmill in good shape so it would continue to pump and keep the stock tank full of fresh water.

In the spiritual realm, Jesus said that the Holy Spirit is like the wind, which is powerful enough to change and benefit lives. We are like windmills; we must rise above earthly things to catch the wind, the power of the Holy Spirit. But in order to have the spiritual posture that can utilize the Spirit's power, we depend on Christ. Without the daily maintenance of forgiveness, we soon become ineffective and dry, causing irritating squeaking noises and eventual breakdown. My friend, rise up and seek the Holy Spirit's presence, and take time with Jesus Christ and His power to change you.

"You must be born again. The wind blows wherever it chooses. You hear its sound but you cannot tell where it comes from or where it is going. So it is with everyone born of the Spirit" (John 3:8).

Distraction

THE RIDE WAS SIMPLE enough for a green two-year-old mare I'd started riding a month before, so it looked like a good progression in her training. But as nightfall was settling in and we headed for home, I sensed the mare tensing up.

We had moved three yearlings out of the manured corrals and "thrown" them into a nearby pasture with other cattle to graze on spring grass. The way home was through a timbered area and crossed a logging road with fresh scoria gravel on it. I told my dog to stay close since this territory was new for the young mare and I knew young horses don't like being alone in timbered areas at nightfall. She was in no mood for surprises.

Suddenly, my not-so-obedient herd dog disappeared—probably chasing a rabbit or getting a new "perfuming" by rolling in some fresh cow manure. Then, just as suddenly, he reappeared, enthusiastically racing along the scoria-covered road for two hundred yards to catch up and then dashing over the edge of the road not twenty feet from the feet of the young mare. The dog's feet on the flakes of scoria caused a loud rattling sound similar to that made by a large rattlesnake. The startling sound and the movement ahead on the road caused the unseasoned mare to lose her composure. She flew into a frenzied "I'm out of here" spooked race that would have put a less-experienced rider on the ground, walking home wondering how to discipline a dog for being a dog. I instinctually fell back on the reins, drawing her up in three strides; we rode home calmly in the twilight.

This herd dog had no inkling of the near wreck that his disobedience caused. He was being carefree and enjoying the interesting and stimulating things around him. Similarly, we often become distracted and then race to catch up and follow Jesus. We have no idea how this may affect people around us. Each of us needs to follow Jesus with His gentle and realistic commands. Following closely is of great value. When Jesus asks us to follow Him, it's not because He wants to spoil our fun; instead He foresees the negative effects of our following at a distance. His desire is to be our loving master, Savior, and friend. Follow Him today and stay close day by day, moment by moment.

"And He [Jesus] said unto another, 'Follow Me' but he said, 'Lord allow me … to go and …'" (Luke 9:59).

The Mark

THE BRANDING CORRAL IS, at first glance, a completely confusing place filled with bellering, milling cattle, a haze of smoke, and a melee of activity, but it is actually quite organized. The branding crew has three tasks: to brand, vaccinate, and castrate the hundreds of calves brought in with the herd. Every one of the men and women knows his or her responsibility.

One particular day at the corral, a dozen riders had started before the crack of dawn, gathering cattle from the surrounding hills. Now three skilled ropers on lathered but quiet horses roped calves and dragged them to the ground crew, who were waiting with the hot irons and the other instruments. It was a well-organized and efficient scene. Hardly a voice was heard over the steady drone of bellering cows calling to their calves; hardly a loop was wasted by the ropers.

While calves being branded have no choice in the matter—they simply trust their mothers as they follow along—we do have a choice. Many of us simply follow the flow of life and hope for good things to happen, but we need to look to God in the events of our lives. He is closer than we often realize. Some of our days are uneventful, while other moments, as with these calves, take on tremendous significance. Calves have no way of knowing the future value of the painful mark being put on them. But, like it or not, we choose our brand. Invest in eternal value by moving toward the loop of God's "branding crew." Make sure your future is in His hands, because He has eternal life planned for you.

"You are not your own for you have been bought with a price therefore glorify God in your body and your spirit which are God's" (1 Corinthians 6:19–20)

Rattlesnake

IT WAS A FAMILIAR sound, yet still startling. My horse stopped dead in his tracks as I scanned the grass and brush immediately in front of us. A rattlesnake was emanating the alarming warning that his space was being invaded and he would certainly bring on consequences that could be deadly. I slowly backed my horse out of the danger zone, dismounted, and tied the gelding to some brush. I pulled my rope off the saddle and cautiously approached the grass where the snake was coiled up and continuing its loud warning. I had seen enough swelled noses and mouths due to snakebites on cattle and horses that I made it a part of my work to eliminate rattlesnakes whenever

I ran into them. Using the honda end of the open loop, I swung it vertically and accurately popped the viper on the head, laying it out flat. With my jackknife, I sliced off its head; I then buried it lest a herd dog or scavenging bird eat it and ingest the venomous fangs. I then tied the dangling, still occasionally rattling, viper to saddle strings and resumed my morning check. It would make a good meal for the barn cats, I thought, and the rattle was big enough to add to my collection.

A spiritual lesson for any follower of Christ: Many spiritual injuries can be averted if we stay alert and courageously move forward in prayer. Our spiritual enemies carelessly signal their presence to a watchful heart.

"Continue in prayer and watch in the same with thanksgiving" (Colossians 4:1).

The Saddle

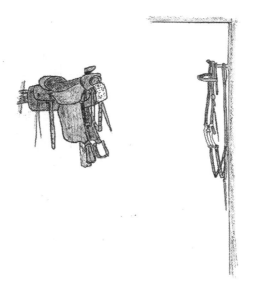

IT WAS NOT AN ordinary saddle—nothing was ordinary at this historic horse ranch—but one would not know that by how it was stored. It was slung on a rack on the back of the saddle shed. It was an A-tree, rough-out, now worn smooth roping saddle with years of wear on it, but it was definitely not plain or ordinary.

The ranch crew had ridden all day to move cattle over a sage-covered ridge to a different pasture. One of the cowhands returning with them to the ranch was riding with painful saddle sores on the insides of his legs; his saddle was so worn out that he needed something better. The foreman noticed his pain and offered the old rough-out saddle collecting dust on the rack. The offer was eagerly accepted, and a price was agreed upon. Suddenly the dust-laden saddle had new attention. It was taken down, cleaned, oiled, checked for sound latigos and given more attention than it had had for years. With an eager smile like a child at Christmas, the cowboy mused over his new possession and rode it with pride and feelings of accomplishment.

Often there are gifts and abilities in each of us that can be ignored for a long time but then drafted into use when a need arises. These can be times of anxiety or exhilaration as we see our potential to be used by God. Most of us do not ever feel useless but just ignored at times. Waiting can be difficult, but the hope of usefulness must always be a part of our faith. Trust in the Lord and know that He desires to use you for His kingdom work.

"… useful to the Master and prepared to do every good work" (2 Timothy 2:21).

A Deep Well

IT WAS A DIFFICULT sight to watch: thirsty cattle in the blistering sun trying to sip a thin film of water off the top of a silted-in waterhole. It was dangerous too; a thirsty cow could get bogged down while trying to reach an unreachable last drink.

Early the next day, the ranch crew arrived with shovels, picks, ropes, and buckets as the hopes for usable water turned into action. The first five or six feet of the thirty-six-inch diameter "well" went without incident. But when buckets and rope were needed to lift the dirt out, things got more difficult for the man in the hole. Once a rock rolled off the heaping bucket and ricocheted down the hole, hitting the digger on the back.

After three days of digging, water started collecting down in the hole and had to be removed before further digging could commence. The mornings began with extracting that water together with mud, muck, and rock. When the well was deep enough, a twenty-foot-long steel culvert with slits cut into its sides on the bottom three feet was inserted into the hole. This allowed clean water to seep through. A crude pump jack was set up with a pipe reaching down into the fresh water seeping into the culvert, providing eight feet of fresh, clean water to pump for thirsty cattle during the drought.

My Christian friend, there is living water inside each of us that believes in Christ, but so much mud and sin must be removed before it is usable to the Holy Spirit to give life to us and others. A deep well is needed to provide adequate water in a drought. None of us knows when spiritual drought and trials will come. Now is the time to dig deep and dredge out unneeded habits and rocks of laziness that hinder. A deep well is also needed for adequate water in demanding times. The Holy Spirit looks out on lives and sees potential for increased love, care, and giving to those in need. Allow, invite, even implore the Holy Spirit to dig deep into your heart and remove that which hinders the flow of life to thirsty people around you.

"The water that I shall give him shall be in him a well of water springing up into eternal life" (John 4:14).

A Lousy Life

AT FIRST, THE BLACK baldy calf didn't attract much attention. Sure, she was the last to mosey up to the feed bunks, but that was not unusual. But then I noticed her alone, looking a little humpbacked. *What is wrong with you?* I thought as I was doing the feeding. It was a hurried morning, so I had only time for a quick trip to the chute. She had no fever, so a quick shot of antibiotics eased my concern as I mounted my horse and headed for another part of the ranch.

Days went by. Often the calves were fed after dark, so the rough-haired heifer went unnoticed. More calves were dumped into the pen, and in the swirl of activities, this calf often stood alone, grinding her teeth in pain and discomfort.

One day as the ranch hands gathered several pens for vaccination and worming, this black baldy heifer was knocked down in the press to exit the feeding pen. I then noticed it was the same problem calf

I had seen two months ago. I quickly dismounted and tried to help her up, but she had no stamina left. I suddenly saw the problem: lice were crawling into her eyes and nose, literally falling off her. *Those stinkin' critters are thick on her; no wonder she's so weak,* I thought.

"Let's get her out of here before she infests the whole feed grounds!" I yelled. My partner slipped a rope around her hind legs, mounted his horse, and dragged her out of the alleyway and into an empty corral. Sadly, she died before dark, her life drained out of her by the blood-sucking lice.

It was a hard lesson for a busy crew that hadn't had time to take care of a small problem. What that black heifer needed was a total dipping or a delousing powder, either of which would have cleansed every square inch.

My friend, each of us, like this black heifer, is in dire need of an all-over cleansing from the draining power of sin that increases day by day and weakens us though others cannot see it. A swirl of dust-making activity may go on around us, but God sees our hopeless future without cleansing through Christ. This world offers token remedies that make us feel as though they are helping, but without a thorough, powerful remedy, our future is no more hopeful than this calf. She had no choice, but we do. Call out to Jesus for hopeful cleansing today. "Though your sins be as scarlet they will be as white as snow, though they be red like crimson, they shall be as wool" (Isaiah 1:18).

Attacker

THE SUN WAS BRIGHT on that cool summer morning with fluffy white clouds floating lazily across the sky. I was on a routine ride to check on the health and numbers of a bunch of black baldy cows and their calves out in a pasture north of the main ranch. I took the opportunity to contemplate the peaceful beauty around me and the fine horse I was mounted on. I never thought to look at the sky immediately above my head, so I was completely surprised and confused when my hat was suddenly knocked off, causing my horse to bolt. Only when I heard the screams and saw the attacking hawk did I begin to understand the unexpected attack that had disrupted my peaceful ride. I then saw the nest she was trying to protect in a tree nearby. The angry bird continued to circle overhead, crying at me with such fury that the peaceful valley was turned into a noisy, unhappy location. I dismounted, picked up my hat, and, smiling at the courage of this attacker, remounted and headed up country.

How often our lives are disrupted by a barrage of thoughts that, like an angry hawk, try to steal our repose. Though outwardly we may appear to be relatively at peace, in our brain a dreadful flood of fears can happen every time certain events or circumstances occur. Events like memories of undesirable happenings, the reoccurrence of a health problem, the death of someone we know, or financial deficits are inevitable. The Bible reminds us that inner peace happens only as we take control of our thoughts and focus on Jesus

Christ. He promises His peace as we live in His forgiveness and love. Daily serenity is maintained as we live in close relationship with Him.

"Surely He will deliver you from the noisome pestilence. He shall cover you" (Psalm 91:3).

Being Wise

MY HEART SANK. I had been hoping for a gift of hard cash, or at least something that had immediate value. Instead I was given a colt, named Tie'um, with the assurance from the giver that it had great potential and was of great value. Others gave me a different story—that the colt would have very little to offer.

After much thought and wisdom from previous experiences I decided to invest time and energy in this unwanted gift. In the process I learned some valuable lessons.

The first was that, especially at the beginning, young colts need to be guarded, since no matter where they are stabled, they are liable to get injured, cut, or torn up by small things, debris that might be lying around. A valuable colt can easily have its whole life's potential crippled and wasted. Young colts can also run off and get lost. Chasing Tie'um in the midst of all my daily chores was all-consuming, and it took great effort to retrieve him. Thus I came to the conclusion that Tie'um needed to be kept in close and not turned out to range.

As the horse matured, I also realized I needed to control that horse and not let it control me. A well-trained horse will not crowd his owner but has learned to follow and wait for his master. Eventually I became wise to the fact that this was not any ordinary gift. The colt had potential to benefit me greatly and to work for me. It was paying off to invest the time it took to train Tie'um, rather than letting him stand around year after year, depleting resources.

"Be careful then how you live, not as unwise people, but as wise, make good use of the time" (Ephesians 5:15,16). Just as I would have been foolish to squander my gift by letting Tie'um go his own way, we often waste our gifts by failing to make good use of our time.

Blockage

IT WAS THE THIRD day that I had seen this scraggly-looking heifer in the same location in a rugged coulee. Upon a closer look, I saw she had strands of grass hanging out of her mouth. I concluded I had to take time out of gathering dry cows out of that pasture to more closely examine that heifer. With very little resistance from her, I was able to rope her and began to pull dry, unmasticated grass out of her mouth. Being careful to pry her mouth open and not get my fingers pinched in her teeth, I looked for some reason the heifer's throat might be blocked. My search was rewarded: just past her tongue, near the entrance to the esophagus, was lodged a short, woody piece of sagebrush stem. With considerable effort on my part, my hand forced down the throat of the struggling, hog-tied young cow, I was able to extract the woody culprit wedged in the heifer's throat.

I stuck the smelly piece of sagebrush wood in my pocket, untied the young bovine, coiled up my ropes, remounted, and headed up country to continue my work. The extra time was well spent; this struggle was life-saving for a cow.

So, too, in life: small things in the wrong place can, after a period of time, have serious consequences. These obstructions will not remove themselves, but we are different from a heifer waiting helplessly for someone with an eye to see our problem. We can choose to ask for God's help. In His mercy, He will come and deliver us from any problem: a habit, an addiction, a harmful thought pattern, or just a negative attitude. But we must ask.

Breaking Trail

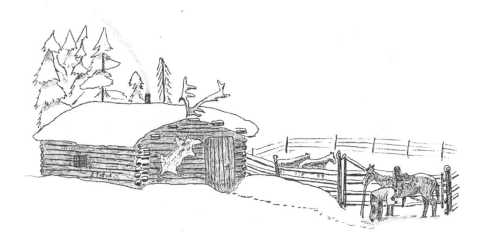

THE COWHAND RODE ONTO a ridge after a fresh fall of snow during the night. Ninety cows were stranded on the ridge, unable to see their way down through a long, steep snowdrift that was three or four feet deep. Instinct told them that they could die in deep snow if they couldn't find solid ground under them to walk out of it.

The cowhand knew that if he could persuade one cow to walk through the heavy snow, the others would follow. He cut out a cow that had an experienced look about her and an appearance of leadership in the pecking order. He rode in front of her and called her to follow. His horse plowed through the drift, breaking a trail for the cows. He rode to level ground and then went back to encourage the designated leader. She resisted slightly but then moved down the trail made by the horse and rider in the deep snow. The shivering, hungry herd now gladly followed the newly anointed leader as she carefully stepped through the deep snow, and they were soon on the feed grounds, where hay and fresh water awaited them.

Christian, others are stranded in lifestyles and habits that keep them from attempting a route to freedom and life. Jesus Christ is nudging you to follow His steps on a trail that leads to fulfillment and abundance. He has "broken trail" for you; now lead others to that trail; they are looking for someone to follow. Be faithful to your calling.

"Then I will teach transgressors your ways" (Psalm 51:13).

Burdens

THE VETERINARY'S WORDS WERE sobering and disheartening. "See how deep these lacerations go into this forearm muscle? The major arteries have been severed, and in just a matter of time, gangrene will set in because this leg no longer has the circulation needed to sustain life in this flesh," he said as he pointed to the wound on the horse's front leg. "At this point, your choices are putting her to sleep or letting her die a slow, painful death."

My friend was sick about the choice and knew he could do neither. Later that afternoon, he asked me, "Do you put horses to sleep?"

"Yes, I guess I've done that when it needs to be done. Why do you ask?"

"I've got this injured mare … the vet says it's my only choice at this point, but I don't have the heart for it. Could you do it for me?"

"Bring the horse here this afternoon, and I'll do it," I replied.

Some things in life are too hard to do by ourselves. We need help with them. An example is facing losses of health or loved ones. Fortunately, we are not alone; if we reach out to others, we can have hope for the future.

"Carry each other's burdens, and in this way you will fulfill the law of Christ" (Galatians 6:2).

Buzzards

THEY WERE UGLY BIRDS, and they had an ugly job to do. They gathered over the dead cow with lustful viciousness to strip the bones clean. The three buzzards slurped up the crawling maggots together with the rank rotting flesh of the carrion that had bloated three days before in the hot sun. The clean-up job was something no one else wanted to do, and these buzzards did it better than anyone else in the world.

One thing buzzards do not do well is plan for the future. An amazing fact is that they need twenty or thirty feet to run before they can lift off into the air for flight. Buzzards are known to land on a carcass without an exit strategy. They apparently never look up when they are feeding. They can be trapped by a three-foot fence.

A lesson for us might be to do our work as best we can, realizing that even if we cannot do it with enthusiasm, we can choose to do it well. However, when we need to rise above the stench and discouragement of problems around us, we need to look up and not get caught by the problems. Only Jesus Christ can help us in the time of spiritual need. He has proven His love by providing eternal life to all that call upon Him. Look up to Him today.

"I will lift up my eyes unto the hills from where my help comes from. My help comes from the Lord which made heaven and earth!" (Psalm 121:1–2).

Close Call

MY HEART WAS POUNDING like a machine gun in combat, and bull snot was dripping off my neck! Had my saddle horn been one inch shorter, my arm might not have caught on it and I might have fallen into the path of an angry bull.

The two-thousand-pound black powder-keg was being reluctantly headed up country at my persistent pressure. Every chance he could, the dusty, manure-smeared bull tried to hide near any trees or patch of Juneberry bushes he could find. With loud hollers, I urged the increasingly irritated bull, snorting and bellowing his resistance, to lumber in the direction I pointed him toward.

Although experienced in this sort of thing, I found myself wishing I had brought along a good herd dog. Especially as I watched this angry beast, inflamed by his persistent pursuer, duck into a patch of brush in which cattle often spent hot, fly-infested afternoons. I briefly wondered if I'd best leave this one be and try again the following day. But the gate into the pasture where I was directing this bull was only a half-mile away, so I decided to make one more try. I cautiously approached the brush, hoping to hear the bull crashing his way out the other side.

Suddenly, a mass of black fury exploded out of the green vegetation toward me! My horse reacted instinctively. Quick on his feet, he spun 180 degrees in a split second and dashed out of harm's way. I was hanging on to his side like a rag doll with the crook of my arm hooked on the saddle horn. During that split second as the horse spun to avoid the mad bull, the bull's head was within inches of this helpless rider, blowing snot into my face as the fast-running horse carried me, dangling, out of the danger zone.

While the snorting bull retreated back into the brush, I pulled myself back into the saddle and took stock of the situation. Had I hit the ground in front of this charging beast, he probably would have seriously injured or even killed me. Although I had not finished the task I had set out to do, I headed home in the heat of the day with a grateful spirit, realizing that someone was watching over me and life is never to be taken for granted.

"For He shall give His angels charge over you, to keep you in all your ways" (Psalm 91:11).

Cookhouse

THERE WAS MERRIMENT AND celebration at the cookhouse that night. It had been an impossibly difficult day. The crew had corralled 1,500 yearlings on a cold, windy day. Though they were shorthanded, it needed to be done, and they had pulled it off; not one yearling was missing after three months of summer grazing. At times like this, the cookhouse at the ranch becomes the center of fulfillment and celebration. The crew celebrated their well-earned victory by eating a good meal together. It felt so good to have hot food, hot coffee, lights, and no wind. They were well aware that their predecessors would probably have eaten beef jerky, soda crackers, and raisins in the dark.

When human beings work together, it can be a place where peace and contentment reign. Celebrations can overcome times when tempers flare, fights break out, and words are spoken that cause hurt and pain—times when the physically strong win and the smaller and weaker must resort to secrecy and conniving to even the score. Human relationships thrive when pride and arrogance are set aside and actual interest in others is cultivated. Our heavenly Father illustrates this in the story of the prodigal son in Scripture. He welcomed back into the family a son returning after wasting his time, money, and life. We can show the same welcome for people who are different from us.

"Let us eat and be merry." (Luke 15:23).

Darkness

WHEN I WALKED UP to the oat shed and unlatched and opened the rickety old door, bright sunlight flooded the room. The light revealed cobwebs and dust, and I could see at least a half dozen rats scampering back to their holes under a small pile of rotting leftover grain. The oat shed was a building that had been completely ignored during the busy summer of cow-work, haying, and harvest. This season of neglect made it a haven for rats and spiders, which thrive on darkness and quiet. Now the oat shed was about to receive its yearly blessing of a new load of freshly harvested oats; dirt and varmints were not welcome.

Darkness, just by itself, is quiet and undisturbed, but when the Lord sends in light, the darkness has to go. Darkness and light cannot mutually coexist, for the one is in opposition to the other. When the Lord Jesus gives to any person His light, it is His will to increase this light within us. He desires for us to separate ourselves from the darkness by receiving what He would give us. The things of this world cannot stand before the light of Jesus, and even the frivolous amusements will scurry into oblivion as we allow our lives to be covered over by a deeper sense of purpose and usefulness in carrying out our lives in obedience and love to our Master. My friend, are you allowing the light into your life? Are you embracing the process that opens you to usefulness to the Master?

"[He] … will bring to light the hidden things of darkness …" (1 Corinthians 4:5).

Deficiency

WHEN I FIRST SAW the strange sight, I was amused, and then I was intrigued. A small bunch of cows were standing in a huddle near a reservoir. It was as if it were a mourning session for a deceased cow from one year ago. As I rode over to investigate further, the sight became even more bizarre: six or seven cows were standing in a circle, each with a bleached cow bone in her mouth, chewing and sucking on it. I chuckled to myself at the rare sight; it was almost as if these cows were putting on a comedy act for a camera crew or a paid audience. Then I noticed something that made me think. The mineral box was empty. I wondered if these cows could be suffering from a mineral deficiency. I'd been told that grass is usually high in calcium but often low in phosphorus. *Is there absorbable phosphorus in bleached cow bones?*

I thought. *Possibly so.* I finished my circle and returned that afternoon with a sack of livestock mineral to fill the trough.

Do we experience spiritual deficiencies? The human heart longs for purpose and feelings of validation. The routine of life without hope for fulfillment and change can cause one to weaken in heart and mind. New opportunities and helpful changes can bring renewed energy and enthusiasm. A life running out of these can become slow and dependent on something from the outside in an attempt to add courage and momentum. Jesus Christ offers an injection of spiritual life that overcomes all deficiencies. Seek Him today for help. In John 10:10, Jesus says, "I am come that they might have life and that they might have it more abundantly."

Don't Turn Back

IT WAS A COLD spring day, and the wind had a chill factor that bit at the nose and ears. Dark clouds hung on the horizon, and the headwind was picking up. I was guiding a small herd of cattle up the narrow trail. Although my dog was doing his best, weaving back and forth, encouraging the stragglers to stay with the herd and not give up because of their weariness, it was clear that the cold headwind was causing the herd to move slower and slower.

Suddenly, the lead cow turned off the road and stood near some brush, facing the herd. Instantly, the leading pairs turned off the road with her, and the entire group stopped. As the overcast sky began to release sleet and light rain, the wind drove it painfully into my face. At first I instructed my dog to go around the right side of the herd to motivate the leading cows to get on the trail again. However, it soon became clear that the effort was hopeless. With the herd dog out of sight, several cows with their calves gathered and began to move down country past me. As I turned back those cows breaking from the herd, I called back my dog. It was time to wait out the strong headwind.

Sometimes there comes a point in our lives when we need to "wait out the headwind". Although time does not always change our circumstances, and although the climate for moving ahead might not change, a pause to regroup our thoughts and reevaluate our goals and direction can be very helpful. "And God is faithful; He will not allow you to be tempted beyond what you can bear" (1 Corinthians 10:13).

So often, our hearts are weak in our faith and trust in Him and His love. As we realize that Jesus Christ paid a great price for us and will not let us go without something, we really need to walk this road of faith. Let us see that His patience with us is one of His many demonstrations of His tremendous love for us. Yield yourself to Him today.

Easy Yoke

THE NORTH WIND WHISTLED down on the feed grounds, where the winter bunch stood humped over their hay with their backs to the icy blast. I had to encourage my team to keep the hay sled moving. The manure piles, which are almost unnoticeable in summertime, become hidden obstacles when frozen and encountered under the freshly blown snow. I had hooked up the team in such a manner that my trusty old horse, Blackey, was pulling over half his share of the load, and his partner, a green sorrel, was practically enjoying the morning feed. It was simply a case of moving the pin in the yoke off dead center to give the sorrel a leverage advantage. At one point, as they crossed a dry creek bed, the snow began to pile up in front of the sled so much that the team's hind feet were churning up piled snow. Blackey's black coat became frosty white, proving he was getting warm during this workout. For the sorrel it was a mild workout, thanks to the uneven yoke. He would be ready to go again tomorrow after we finished the feeding and headed for the barn.

Jesus Christ invites us to yoke up with Him in a restful life of serving Him. He said, "Come unto me all you who labor and are heavy laden and I will give you rest. Take My yoke upon you and learn of Me, for I am meek and humble and you shall find rest unto your souls. For My yoke is easy and My burden is light" (Matthew 11:28–30).

Empty Well

MY HORSE HAD OBVIOUSLY heard something; he kept looking to the east. It was a quiet day with no wind, so the slightest sound could be heard a distance away. I had veered off my usual circle to take in the sight of an old homestead up in the pine trees. As I rode through the overgrown yard and observed the few run-down buildings (the hard work of someone in another time), I noticed nothing unusual at first. But as I turned in that direction, I observed the barely noticeable outcropping of brick from an old well. No doubt something was in there, as my usually compliant horse refused to stride up to the hole.

As I dismounted and walked toward the well, I could clearly hear labored breathing. About eight feet down in the four-foot diameter hole, tangled in discarded, rusty barbed wire, was a scratched-up, dehydrated yearling bull. He'd probably been pushed in by an older bull.

"I'll be back", I said, "but I'll need help to get you out, so don't die on me in the meantime." It was hours later before I was able to make it back with a tractor, but he was still alive. Wasting no time in starting the rescue effort, I crawled down into the hole. With much effort, having to work around the rusty wire, I managed to get a heavy rope around the mid-section of the dying bull. The tractor easily lifted the half-ton yearling out. The rest was up to him. I set out a bucket of water to give the dehydrated beast a limited supply of much-needed liquid, and I planned to check on the reviving bull in the morning.

What an irony; a former source of life-giving water becoming a death trap to an animal, I thought. The Scripture talks about people who can become as "wells without water" (2 Peter 2:17). At one time, "out of their innermost being flowed rivers of living water" (John 7:38). Adversities of life can silt in, cut flow to, and just plain dry up a spiritual life. The Holy Spirit is available to rehydrate and cause purified water to flow again. Invite Him to keep you flowing today.

Endurance

As I CAREFULLY REMOVED the caked shoes from another horse in the winter string, I had to muse about endurance. The shoes had served well to keep the footing of the horse and protect its rider during a part of the winter. Because of their hardness, the shoes would be good for yet another winter. Horseshoes allow a horse's feet to endure the hammering of rocks and frozen ground. They do not break or bend or yield to an adversary that would crack and tatter an unprotected hoof.

What makes people hardy and made of stern stuff? Some might venture the answer is in proper upbringing that teaches one to courageously face challenges and never give up. Others say it must be in certain genes or favorable bloodlines. We see strong and indomitable people in every culture and pioneers can be found in any location on this planet. Although the lap of luxury does not usually afford the elementary iron for the upbringing of a strong and enduring life, a person's choices move them in the direction of victory over seemingly insurmountable odds. Hardness hardens; antagonism, rightly responded to, can solidify. Trials of life will inure and confirm. How commonly it has happened that people who in soft circumstances have been weak and irresolute were hardened into fruitful decisions by the ministry of antagonism and pain.

May the Lord temper us for life's difficulties and shape us to fit the place He has put us in this life.

"Endure hardness as a good soldier of Jesus Christ" (2 Timothy 2:3).

Find Pasture

THERE WAS A SMILE on my face as I flung the gate open after dismounting and carefully untwisting the wire that had secured the gate all winter and spring. Behind me was the winter feedlot, and ahead were new growth, new horizons, and hope for change. As I stepped through the open gate, I had to step out of the way of the older stock animals who were crowding through, manure still caked on their hindquarters from a confined winter in the drylot. By the way they forged ahead down the trail, it was obvious they remembered green grass and all that goes with it. But the calves with fresh brands and no memory of the previous summer approached the open gate more cautiously, unsure of new freedom.

Much like these calves, we embrace familiar ways and hesitate to tread on new, untried turf. There are times when caution and conservatism are the necessary direction, but then there are seasons of change, when risk is the key to appropriate action. Just as the smile on the face of the one opening the gate indicates his pleasure in the scene he brought about, so also our heavenly Father smiles at the release we experience in Christ. We can experience new freedoms as we walk through the open gate. Forge ahead, Christian, past obstacles that have held you back and hemmed you during the winter of your life. New horizons and growth await you as surely as the promises from Christ are true.

"Go in and out and find pasture" (John 10:9).

Follow

I WAS ONE OF the two riders whose job it was that day to head a small herd of cows with newborn calves up country toward a gate one mile away. It was a happy time to get out of those mucky corrals and into some open country, even though leaving the security of the calving sheds was not easy. This was a season that could peril new life should a spring storm blow in.

There was another danger, and to avoid this, we stopped the herd often. Newborn calves are prone to panic if, after too much time and distance, they lack a mother's reassuring love and attention. Instinct tells them (either mother or baby) that if they are separated, they should return to the last place of nursing. In other words, they will head back to familiar surroundings. I and the other rider both had seen "wrecks" while moving cattle because of this. To avoid this, we stopped the herd often to allow the mothers and babies to "mother up" at strategic times.

A spiritual lesson can be taken from this if we heed Job's exhortation (Job 12:7): "But ask now the beasts and they shall teach thee." How often we are tempted to return to old habits, routines, relationships, and places when life becomes difficult and insecure and we're not really sure of the outcome. Jesus Christ, our only source of eternal life, is ahead of us, leading us on to new places and experiences. But when we cannot see Him or hear Him, we are tempted to return to the old. Our past is familiar and comfortable, while the future is often fearful and undesirable, filled with unknowns. As much as we'd like to stay where we are, or even return to the past, Jesus Christ leads us forward and has promised to never leave us. We need to follow and press into him in obedience. He invites us to follow Him.

"He that follows Me shall not walk in darkness but shall have the light of life" (John 8:12).

Good Water

DIGGING A DEEP, EXPENSIVE well was a gamble but worth the try. The rancher had to do something. He was not able to graze a large portion of his ranch because the limited water available was so bitter that cattle could not drink it.

Water that is pure and carries with it no aftertaste of minerals or bitterness is of great value to livestock owners. Lactating cows will drink more than usual and thus provide more milk for their calves, which will, in turn, grow faster than normal and remain strong in times of stress. Feedlot cattle eat more than usual and gain valuable pounds faster than normal if they have good free-choice water available to them.

The rancher had long since abandoned an old well producing bitter water and now was hauling good water to several outlying areas. He knew it was not adequate, since the tanks were always empty when he arrived with his truck and tank of water.

So the day came for the risky project. The drilling went well for the first two days. They were tiring, stressful days with sleepless nights for the rancher. At last the driller hit water, and before the pump that would put out clean water was installed, the rancher tasted the silty fluid. The water smelled of sulfur, but it was drinkable.

"It's not ideal, but this is as deep as we'll go," the rancher said, resigning himself. "It'll be better for the cattle than drinking mud in the slew.

Sometimes in life, although we try our best, we need to settle for less than best. But this is not so in the spiritual realm. Jesus Christ promises us perfect spiritual water that will cause us to never thirst again. Like the rancher that had to compromise, we often settle for a shallow spirituality that we think we can survive on. Jesus says we're to "seek and we will find" (Matthew 7:7).

"Whoever drinks of the water that I shall give him, shall never thirst again … but the water that I shall give him shall be in him a well of water springing up into everlasting life" (John 4:14).

Grass

GRASS IS AN AMAZING thing. So colorful, so soft, it tears easily, crushes in a horse's mouth. When green and moist, it stains your hand or jeans and is sharply fragrant. It is tender and easily eaten by livestock; even a week-old calf or foal can pinch it off and taste it. Yet it may withstand devastating winds, stubbornly clinging to the ground, apt to cover any hillside or valley. When dry in the hot summer and subjected to flame, it can burn so swiftly and ferociously that one has to run for cover and safety. Unless the snow packs it down, it remains forage for livestock all winter until new grass comes in spring.

Some say grass is the healing of the earth's surface. It covers over tracks, ruts, and gorges in the terrain from the year before. Trails that killed the grass in years before grow over. Mistakes, poor choices of travel, and the tracks of mankind's vehicles—all healed by grass.

God's love is like that. It provides sustenance for the weakest of all yet withstands the strongest words of adversity. It can feel the hottest spiritual renewal and yet sustains through the coldest spiritual season. When allowed to grow, it heals the worst injustices of mankind and covers the ugliest actions of thoughtless and angry people. No matter what our conditions today, we need God's powerful love expressed in Jesus Christ.

"Nothing ... will be able to separate us from the love of God that is in Christ Jesus our Lord" (Romans 8:39).

Healing

IT WAS LATE OCTOBER when I paused my dun horse and observed the dried grass that was thickly covering the scar of that day gone by. Could it have been only last spring, that day that is still drilled in my mind? The painful memory swept over me.

A set of portable corrals had been set up in that location. Six seasoned cowboys had been sorting 370 pregnant cows on what started out to be a beautiful, early spring day. Then the wind, rain, and snow moved in, and with it the cutting sounds of a boss who ridiculed the younger riders for not dressing for the weather. The misery was palpable and visible as those cows and riders dug up the muddy ground, scarring the sod till there was not a blade of winter grass inside those corrals.

When they had finished the cut, the riders were assigned to take the herds separate ways. The two hands left took down the corrals in the mud, and all left for the ranch.

Just as grass heals scars in the sod, time has a way of healing painful memories. The deeper the gouging pain, the longer it takes to heal. Life has a way of covering over the past, yet some pain never seems to go away. Only the love of God applied to our lives covers some pain and memories.

"To everything there is a season, a time for every purpose under heaven: … a time to heal" (Ecclesiastes 3:1, 3).

Hope

THE NEWBORN FOAL, IF well cared for, is soon scampering over the spring grass with not a care in the world, probably confident that life can hardly get better. He is completely unaware that a small change in his circumstances could be life threatening. A sudden attack from a predator or the injury or death of its dam seem obvious, but even harassment from other older horses, or a collision with a barbed-wire fence, can change the future and vitality of a healthy foal. The resultant stress on a colt can become a life-and-death matter. Nurture and care by a watchful mother, on the other hand, brings hope by making the colt's life carefree.

Hope for the future is precious to all living creatures. So often that hope is tied to positive circumstances around us. God has promised to supply all that we need to have a future and hope. Seek His presence today for health and life in Christ. Your future is on His mind.

"'For I know the plans that I have for you,' declares the Lord, 'plans to prosper you and not to harm you, plans to give you hope and a future'" (Jeremiah 29:11).

Life

A living dog is better than a dead lion.
—Ecclesiastes 9:4

THE WRITER OF ECCLESIASTES tells us that life, even in its humblest form, is superior to death. A living dog keeps better watch than a dead lion and is of more service to his master. If both were alive, the lion would be stronger and more able to overcome those around him, win every fight, and satisfy every selfish need. But, as it is, life is always preferred over death, despite all other things seeming to be what they are.

On the ranch, the most common-bred ranch horse, while still living, is of greater value than the high-priced, award-winning quarter horse or crown-winning thoroughbred that has just died, though the deceased horse may possess power, recognition, and beauty. The ranch hand who still has his health and life is more to be envied than the wealthy landowner who has suddenly passed away.

In the spiritual realm, it is better to be least in the kingdom of heaven than the greatest out of it. The weakest, most despised person with the life of Christ flowing through him is better off and in a more desirable place than another without Christ, though the latter may possess power, recognition, and beauty. The poorest prayer is infinitely preferred over talented oration; the most meager attempt to serve God is better than religious exercises that have no wisdom. In all that we do, if we are energized by the Holy Spirit, nothing is worthless but rather alive. At the same time, our grandest performances and our greatest accomplishments, if lacking a yielding to Christ, are like a dead carcass—motionless, powerless, with a stench that draws flies and vultures—a pitiful sight in the eyes of God. Quicken us, make us alive, oh God.

Little Things

THE MASSIVE BULL WAS hardly able to walk. Why? He had foot rot caused by bacteria smaller than the eye can see. A thoroughbred race horse was unable to race because he had a miniscule piece of gravel lodged in his hoof. Other tiny objects can cause big problems: a little dust can destroy a wheel bearing, a grain of sand can hinder one's vision, a little thorn in the hand can cause much suffering.

"Little foxes spoil the vines" (Song of Solomon 2:15b), and in the same way, little sins do mischief to the tender heart. A great sin cannot destroy a Christian, but a little sin can make him miserable. It is easy to recognize the guilt we feel after committing flagrant sins, but the uneasiness and lack of peace that result from "little" sins are often overlooked as a part of life—but they are not a part of the believer's intimate walk with Christ. Just as a small infection can sideline the ruling bull of the rangeland, or a tiny bit of gravel eventually lames the fastest horse, so, in time, do the overlooked "little sins" eventually work deep into the heart to sideline the believer in Christ. If you would see Christ's love and walk with Him, take heed to "the little foxes that spoil the vines." Jesus invites you to go with Him and take those foxes, bringing them into captivity. Let Him assist you in routing out the little things that bring great hindrances.

"If you keep My commandments, you shall abide in My love, even as I have kept My Father's commandments and abide in His love" (John 15:10).

Look for Spring

WAS IT MY IMAGINATION, or was the frost a little heavier on the ground than it was the day before? *Wasn't the ice on the water tank a bit thicker than yesterday's ice?* I wondered. As I tucked my hands into my pockets and rode out of the corral and into the open pasture, memories of the biting cold of past winters began to surround me. It was another day looking for missing cows that needed to be relocated before winter blew in. Every morning, these small hints gave way to thoughts that the season of summer had long since ended. Gloomy anticipations began to push at me like an old haystack leaning on a weak fence.

I have to ask this question with the psalmist: "Why go I mourning?" (Psalm 42:9). Can you find a reason you are mourning instead of rejoicing? Who told you the night would not turn into day? Who told you that the discontent of fall would proceed from frost to frost, from ice to snow, from colder wind to deeper snow and more deep snow? Do you not know that spring follows winter? That day follows night? Have you forgotten that for everything there is a season, and that the seasons change? Then cling to hope and always know that God will never fail you. Remember that God loves you regardless of the circumstances.

Springtime, though seemingly a long way off, will come. The grass will turn green again. You will, amid the splendors of eternity, forget the cold winds of trial and only remember them with a heart that blesses the God who led you through them.

Proud Flesh

PATCHES

HORSES ARE BEAUTIFUL ANIMALS—AMAZINGLY strong but thin-skinned. A cut to a horse's lower leg, where very little muscle or fat lies between the skin and bone, can become a frustrating injury to heal. The skin pulls apart, and it's virtually impossible to suture. This healing process can be deceptive. At first the injury appears to be healing well; the fresh pink tissue grows rapidly. But then this new granulation tissue keeps growing, becoming ugly and lumpy, rising above the healthy flesh around it. "Proud flesh" is what this scar tissue is called.

Proud flesh is really a false, or at least inadequate, healing. It becomes a potential problem when it grows unchecked. At its worst, in crucial areas, proud flesh can inhibit a horse's movement and even result in lameness.

Many of us have experienced a spiritual "proud flesh" as we've tried to quickly heal a deep wound in our lives. Possibly in an attempt to protect ourselves from further pain, our pride reacts to intrusions with bitterness, self-pity, blame, resentment, and guilt. All of these can prevent a healthy healing and tend to increase with time.

Once proud flesh develops in an injured horse, it can be surgically removed, but this process usually needs to be repeated numerous times. Most horse owners find it more effectual to patiently cleanse the wound and treat it with a granulation tissue–removing ointment day after day. It's a long, painful process, and it requires patience, perseverance, and a lot of time. The horse experiences pain and often vigorously resists the owner's attempts to doctor the wound, seeing its handler as the source of its pain.

Our reactions aren't much different: "Oh God, how could you let this happen to me? Where were you on that fateful, painful day?" Yet healthy healing can only occur as we regularly come before the Lord, confessing our pride and self-adequacy, asking Him to remove that which hinders His Spirit from healing the deep wounds in our lives. The apostle John communicated this very well when he said, "If we confess our sins, He is faithful and just to forgive our sins and cleanse us from all unrighteousness" (1 John 1:9). Jesus Christ is the source of complete healing, and He invites us to let Him further that process in us today.

Trust

IN THE ROUND PEN, the horse hand had the wild buckskin roped and snubbed, but it would not take a single step forward. Whether it was instinct or just raw fear of this leather-clad rider, the gelding fought the rope (and later the halter) to distance himself from the two-legged human, no matter what the pain. Day after day the buckskin sucked back on the rope and would not take the slightest step toward the bowlegged cowboy. He did not realize that just one step forward would ease the pain and actually make his life better and assure him a useful future.

How many times we refuse to come close to a God that totally has our best interests in mind. He proved this by purchasing us through Christ Jesus, and He has plans to prosper and help. Now it is our turn to trust Him that He will help us and not harm us.

"Let us draw near to God with a sincere heart in full assurance of faith" (Hebrews 10:22).

Polluted Well

"SOMETHING'S WRONG WITH THAT water," yelled my partner. "Let's taste it." It was a sweltering, hot day near the end of June, and we had just finished an early morning circle at noon. We had stopped at the well on the south end of section 54 to check the fence and to water our horses. An instant after the thirsty horses gulped water from the stock tank, they bobbed their heads, letting the water fly out. They tried drinking again but showed their distaste by curling up their noses and lips. The water was apparently undrinkable. When we tasted it, sure enough, it was bitter and rank.

When we pulled off the rotting planks that covered the shallow well and peered into the musty-smelling cavern, the problem with the water became obvious. A shaft of sunlight revealed a large drowned rat. He must have been trying to navigate the well casing for a drink and slipped and fell into the water. Now, a week or two later, the carcass was covered with putrefying bacteria, and it was as big as a fuzzy, small dog.

"We've got to get that culprit out," the older cowboy declared as he began to rig up a rope loop to stand in. I faced my task with a branch in hand and a determined look on my face as I was lowered the fourteen feet to the water. I carefully scooped up the putrefying, polluting carcass and began my ascent. Here's where things got difficult; the carcass was so fragile that a slight bump on the edge of the well casing sent pieces of carrion back into the water. I moaned but knew it was hopeless—my "rescue" was unsuccessful.

"We'll come back tomorrow with a bucket," said my partner. We returned early the next day with a bucket to scoop up the polluting, decaying flesh of the varmint. Then we pulled the plug on the stock tank and ran the pump all that day until pure, fresh water returned once again.

Christian, our hearts can harbor many things. Anger, bitterness, or lust can fester inside our hearts and will affect others around us. If we are willing to confess it to Christ, He promises to cleanse us from any "rat" lodged in our hearts.

"If we confess our sins He is faithful and just to forgive us our sins and cleanse us from all unrighteousness" (1 John 1:9).

Porcupine

I FELT SORRY FOR the new mother when I saw her with a face full of porcupine quills. The cow probably had great mothering abilities and was, no doubt, proud of her new calf born just the day before. But she had definitely overreacted to the porcupine.

The porcupine is no predator and simply goes about eating tree bark, twigs, and other forage. There is no way it can be a threat to a calf. But its actions had been misread by the overzealous cow, and her reaction had resulted in much pain and a face full of painful quills. As difficult as it would be, the quills had to be extracted, because decreased grazing would reduce her production of much-needed milk for her young calf. Because it was a two-person process, I returned the next day with another rider to head and heel the cow for the quill extraction process.

How often, if the power is ours, we overreact to others who appear weaker and we find ourselves in fights and arguments that would be better off left alone. Living peacefully with others takes courage and discernment. Wisdom moves us in that direction.

"Starting a quarrel is like breaching a dam; so drop the matter before a dispute breaks out" (Proverbs 17:14).

Repairs

"WILL IT HOLD CATTLE?" My boss's question confronted me that night in the bunkhouse. I had spent all day fixing a run-down fence that had not held cattle for years, getting ready for ninety-six pairs to be turned out into that section until the fall gathering. Sweat dripped off the brim of my old, dust-stained black hat as I pulled the wires tight on a gate I'd just patched together. Old barbed wire can be detestable stuff to work with, but I untangled it and spliced dozens of broken pieces together. I was careful not to stretch some hills too tight, lest the rusty wire break. Repairing the old certainly was less costly than building new fence, but the results were questionable. The boss had sent me to repair the fence and was now questioning me.

"You know those cows," I replied. "Maybe it will hold, but if there's good pickins on the other side, maybe not. The fence is average; some parts are weak, but in other stretches, I put in all new wire where there was none."

Anger showed on the boss's face. "You might as well not have repaired it at all. If there's even one opening or weak area, those cattle will be sure to find it, and they'll spill out. Surely you know that a fence must be tight and strong all the way or it's worthless."

Some people pride themselves in doing pretty well on the whole. They only occasionally get angry and swear they only have a minor lust problem or only occasionally over drink. They try to be kind to the poor if they think of it or have time. My friend, what the ranch boss could not overlook, neither will the Lord overlook on the day of judgment. Trusting in Christ is our only hope.

"Not of works lest any man should boast, for we are His workmanship created in Christ Jesus" (Ephesians 2:9–10).

Salt

You are the salt of the earth.
—Matthew 5:13

THE FLIES SWARMED AROUND my face as I opened the fast-becoming-"ripe" calf hide, which I'd skinned off a dead calf just two days before. It had been on the barn floor, and now I spread it out on the grass so the sunlight could get at it while I spread salt on the raw side. I was amused that the rank smell seemed to dissipate as the newly-hatched maggots tried their best to crawl off this tasty plate of delicacy. Just a light sprinkle of salt totally and quickly changed the minds of these destructive blowfly larva, and they left a valuable object alone.

My thoughts reviewed the life cycle of the flies as I worked on the hide. Blowflies are able to smell an open, festering wound on a cow or horse from miles away. Some of them had decided that this hide, skinned off a dead calf just two days before, would make a fine meal for their young. They'd laid thousands of eggs on it, and the resultant maggots fed on it for days, trying to grow to maturity. If they had finished growing, they would then have crawled off into the dirt, burrowed in, and molted into flies, which would surface and fly away to continue the cycle.

I smiled to myself, feeling victory over a destructive, yet natural, force on the range. I didn't understand all the chemistry details of sodium chloride and osmosis and how it "does a job" on the maggots and yet doesn't ruin the calf-hide. But I knew it worked and this cowboy liked things that work.

Salt has been used to locate cattle in slightly used rangeland, because cows will walk miles to a saltlick. I mused about the value of salt: it is used to drive off a destructive force on the rangeland, and also used to draw in a most valuable commodity.

Christian, Jesus called you the salt of the earth, so never forget that there is a power working in you—the Holy Spirit—and through your submission to Him, the forces of darkness and hell must leave and the grace and love of God are directed into your life, family, and situation.

Showers

I will send down showers in season; there
shall be showers of blessing.
—*Ezekiel 34:26*

ALL OF US KNOW how much the land needs rain. The rangeland will never produce grazeable forage without rain. The farmer may work the land, breaking up the hard, dry clods and planting his seed, but what can he do without rain? Not only is rain needed, but it is also needed in good season. Unless it comes during the critical growing season and before the harvest, it will not do the good it is hoped for. After a long summer drought, a heavy rain during or after harvest is not a blessing, as it only brings a bumper crop of fall weeds for the farmer. The grazing land needs more than a shower; it needs a "soaker"—a week of continuous showers. We need rain that will fill reservoirs, make the creeks run full, and raise the subsurface water table.

So also it is in the spiritual realm. We can put forth our best efforts, but we labor in vain until God showers the needed grace upon us; as a plenteous shower, it comes down with salvation. Is your season today, my friend, a place of spiritual lack and drought? Then this is a season for showers. Is yours a season of heaviness and windswept turbulence? Then this is a season for showers. He gives grace not only for conversion but for comfort as well. And so the promise to our spirits is a plenteous grace—not just for a few drops, or even a shower, but also for "showers of blessing." We need His abundant grace that we may endure difficulties and trials, to preserve us through this life and at last land us in heaven. Look up today, as a parched plant, to receive a heavenly watering.

Solid Footing

… that those things which cannot be shaken may remain.
—Hebrews 12:27

IT WAS A SICKENING sight: ten cows were frozen in the ice. It was a midwinter day, and I had spotted them near a large reservoir. I had been sent out to bring these renegades in. Nearly a dozen cows had managed to avoid the fall gather and strayed to tough it out far from the haystacks and feed grounds of the main herd. The story, as I read it from the ice of the reservoir, was that those range cows had come down for a badly needed drink. A cold snap had frozen over the spring-fed side of the water hole where they were used to drinking. The cows must have pushed out onto the ice, breaking through where it was too deep to climb out. Some ice holds you up, and some doesn't; these bovines could not tell the difference.

There are many things in our lives at the present moment that cannot hold us up, and as believers in Christ, we must not put our trust in these. There is nothing stable beneath these rolling skies; change is written upon all things.

Stick to It

"I QUIT!" SAID THE cowhand. "I don't need to put up with a boss who has no appreciation for my hard work and horse know-how."

"There's plenty of other fellers waiting to take your place," said his friend in dry thoughtfulness, though he hated the thought of his friend leaving the ranch. "Actually, any scumbag, rat, or skunk can back down from a fight and go off by himself. It's the ones with depth and a clean record that can face a situation and stick it out when they don't feel they're getting treated with enough applause and respect."

"After that dispute yesterday over being late," said the hand who was ready to quit, "I just don't have respect for him anymore."

"We all could use a little more affirmation and appreciation," said the friend, "but I've found that when I'm accusing others of not seeing my abilities and skills, it's usually 'cause I've turned into a high-headed horse with no plans of yielding to anyone around me. Times I've quit a situation or job, now looking back; I can see that I always quit too soon. Had I stuck it out a little longer, I'd have seen some rewards I was hoping for, but I let pride rear its ugly head, and I was gone. I sure do regret some of those times now."

Jesus Christ, our example, demonstrated a life bent on following through even when the going got tough. Quitting was not in His personality. He showed incredible courage when he faced his ultimate test—the cross. Rethink your plans today; God gives strength and courage to face difficult times in life.

"Not my will, but yours be done" (Mark 14:36).

Storm

THE SECOND DAY OF a terrific northerner was even worse than the first. Even old-timers called it a blizzard they would remember. The wind was strong enough to roll hay out from under a cow's nose and dissipate it before she could eat but a few bites, and the temperature was thirty-five below zero. Cows bunched together so closely that the thirteen inches of snow that fell that night left piles on the backs of cattle like a white blanket. Breathing in that cold wind caused ice to build up over their noses like ice beards that left a cow looking like a grotesque, ghostlike animal with a foot of snow frozen to her back, neck, and head. Their ears were almost invisible behind a block of ice hanging down six to eighteen inches, sometimes curved forward like an ugly hook.

Even though I was bundled up and had on thick mittens, I could still feel the icy wind and had to tell myself to keep moving. After distributing the hay as best I could, I got out of the wind and mounted my trusty horse to move the cows out of the bed-grounds and to the hay. After observing a bull and a dozen cows unable to open their mouths, simply standing and forlornly watching the others enthusiastically devouring hay, I decided to see if I could break off those ice beards.

I slowly moved the disheartened "ghosts" toward the barn, where I put them into a narrow alleyway. By leaning through the corral rail with a hammer and taking care not to bruise an already tender nose,

I was able to break off the ice beards. Allowing the cattle to eat and drink once again probably preserved their lives.

They would not suffer the fate of other cattle I heard about later: being cut up with chainsaws by city folk who took the frozen beef, leaving the other half still standing upright along the road.

Christian, the chilling trials of life can push one to despondency when the end of the trail seems to loom in the unforeseen future. One must hold to God's promise that "God is faithful who will not allow you to be tempted beyond that you are able but with the temptation allow a way of escape that you may be able to bear it" (2 Corinthians 10:13). The Holy Spirit may chop off a heavy encumbrance today that hinders your life, or tomorrow winds of adversity will subside. Still, endurance is of great need, and Christ is an example of this. "For consider Him that endured such contradiction of sinners against Himself, lest you be wearied and faint in your minds" (Hebrews 12:3). Respond to His voice and invitation to you today. "Come unto me all you that labor and are heavy laden and I will give you rest" (Matthew 11:28).

Strip Off

Let us strip off and throw aside every encumbrance – unnecessary weight – and that sin that so readily clings to and entangles us.
—Hebrews 12:1 AMP

"Why did I bring all of this along?" the rider asked aloud, in between curses, as he attempted to untangle his two packhorses.

The day had started out well. A beautiful, inviting valley lay before him. He was feeling good about deciding to go. It was the kind of place that he'd been looking for, and he anticipated the discoveries that awaited him there. Suddenly he had to pause on the trail before moving down off the hillside, because there seemed to be a disturbance up ahead. As he moved down country to take a closer look, he realized that his string of packhorses had gotten tangled up with each other. Two had "stepped through their ropes," and another had managed to pull loose from the one in front of her and head back down the trail, completely free of her traces.

The rider showed his chagrin as he attempted to untangle the confusion and cursed the things that had held him back. He realized he had only himself to blame for taking so much with him.

Before we laugh at the rider's incompetence, let us see ourselves at the onset of a new year. We anticipate the things before us, but many times we, too, need some help to rearrange things in order to move ahead. Jesus, in His discernment, points out that much of what we continue to carry with us from the past is not necessary at all;

in fact, it needs to be left behind at the foot of a tree—Calvary. He invites us at the beginning of this new year to "strip off" and throw aside every hindrance and weight that is slowing us down on the trip of life. We need to let Him step into our tangled lives and rearrange things according to His plan.

Summer Heat

THE BLISTERING HEAT WAS relentless as the horizon vibrated with heat waves, distorting anything that moved. Every animal and living thing on the prairies sought refuge in the shade of a tree or bush, or even underground if possible. At times, the western hills seemed motionless under the tyrannical oppression of a master that no one could defy. All retreated and hid from its dehydrating and withering rays.

Only six months before, this blasting enemy, the sun, was a friend that lured everyone out into the open to bask in its friendly, warming rays. How can one's attitude change so drastically toward something that remains the same from day to day?

Our circumstances can cause us to seek God, whom at one time we might have done anything to avoid thinking about, hearing about, or reading about. During a life-threatening illness or following the death of a loved one, we might suddenly find ourselves praying. Circumstances have a way of changing our needs, and we act accordingly. We change, but God, like the sun, is unchanging. He says, "I Am the Lord; I change not" (Malachi 3:6). He offers us life whether we feel we need Him or not. Regardless of our feelings, we do need Him. He is there, offering help as the seasons of our lives change. He waits for us to ask for His help.

"Fear not, I will help you" (Isaiah 41:13).

The Hunt

It was November. The leaves had almost all fallen off the trees, and the air was crisp with the foreshadowing of snow. The lone rider saw and felt none of this. He was hunting for one thing: a healthy buck to bring home for food. He'd spent the spring hunting for young heifers with new calves who needed help. All summer he had been on the lookout for calves that had strayed or had pinkeye, bulls that were out of place, and yearling calves that had foot rot. Sometimes his hunt focused on the fences, looking for places that needed mending. Some days he looked at all the water holes, noting the ones that had dried up. Now it was November; the cattle were all safe in a pasture close to the ranch, and he was blind to anything but deer sign: their haunts and their bedding-down places.

Many of us enjoy searching for an addition to our collection, rummaging through stores or catalogues for a favorite item of clothing, tack, or an unusual antique or treasure. A universal game children play is hide-and-seek. All our lives we enjoy one type of hunting or another. What if we could refocus that passion and energy to hunt for a new understanding of God and His love for us? Some of us might think that endeavor is a fruitless effort or a waste of time, but God Himself promises otherwise.

"You shall find Me when you search with all your heart" Jeremiah 29:13.

The value of that kind of hunt can be life changing. Jesus Christ spoke of those that find Him. Nothing compares to the value of time spent hunting for Him!

"When a man found it … in his joy went and sold all that he had and bought the field" (Matthew 13:44).

Patience

His name shall be called Wonderful, Counselor, the mighty God.
—Isaiah 9:6b

A SMALL HERD OF cows waited briefly at the gate on the road leading
to the home ranch. A rider, over a mile back, tried to hurry the
stragglers as the cold north wind pelted snow out of a darkening
December sky. The older cattle waited patiently at the gate, knowing
the cowboy would come and open the way for them. But some of the
younger cows began to drift down the fence line in the direction of
the feed grounds, hoping in their impatience to find another way.

There are choices before us continually in our earthly pilgrimage,
situations in which we need counsel and advice. We can go to our
Lord Jesus Christ and say to Him, "My Lord, I am ignorant, now
what am I to do? You are my counselor. Please show me clearly how

to act in these circumstances." You need never take a step in the dark. Wait until you have light. Wait until He opens the way for you. Others may pass you in a seemingly right direction, but if you patiently wait, believing, expectant, you will find that waiting is not in vain and that the Lord will prove Himself a counselor both wise and good.

Under Cultivation

You are God's cultivated field.
—1 Corinthians 3:9

THE HEART OF EVERY believer is Christ's field or garden. He bought it with His precious blood, and He enters it and claims it as His own. A field or garden implies separation: it is not open range, wilderness, or common ground, but it is fenced in. It is set apart for special cultivation and protection from grazing livestock. Great effort, expense, and care have been given to break up common sod to bring it into production. Would that we could see the wall of separation between godly living and the world made stronger. Surely it grieves and saddens the heart of God to hear us saying, "Well, there is no harm in this or that," seeing how far we can go in worldly conformity.

A field or garden is a place of beauty. Many a rancher's or homesteader's wife maintained her sanity by gazing at the beauty of a productive green garden amid a dusty and empty prairie. It far surpasses the wild, uncultivated, brush-covered sod for lush greenery and variety. The genuine Christian must seek to be more excellent in his life than the best moralist, because Christ's garden ought to grow the best produce and flowers in all the world. Even the best is poor compared to what Christ deserves; let us not put Him off with withering and stunted plants. The richest, choicest, and even rarest crops, produce, and flowers ought to grow in the place that Jesus calls His own.

His cultivated field or garden is a place of growth. Christians are not to remain undeveloped or stunted in their growth or productivity. We should grow in grace and in the knowledge of our Lord and Savior Jesus Christ. Growth should be rapid and continual where Jesus is the husbandman and the sweet showers of His grace water His fields each day. If it is "God who gives the increase" (1 Corinthians 3:7), then we know that each of us, as a believer, has all that is needed to stay in a pattern of growth and productivity. Let your heart become a "cultivated field" that Christ comes to with pleasure and approval.

Winter Thaw

IN SNOW COUNTRY, A break in the usual cold-and-snow routine of winter is welcome but can have undesirable results. Ranchers work all summer putting up hay with the plan to feed it to their livestock during the winter months. Every livestock owner plans for a long winter but hopes for a short, mild one. Despite subzero temperatures or deep snow, hay needs to be fed and frozen creeks or water tanks need to be opened for livestock. A thaw in midwinter comes almost every year, but there's no guarantee of how long it will last or what the result will be. A respite from the bitter cold is enjoyed by man and beast alike, but the most dreaded result is ice. When snow melts and then refreezes, it can cause all kinds of havoc. This crust of ice on snow, if thick enough, can hinder wintering horses from pawing their way to grass under the snow. It can be as sharp as glass, cutting the feet of cattle and horses that attempt to walk on the crust and break it. A thaw that starts out with rejoicing can leave disappointment in its wake.

Here is a spiritual lesson: we can hope for a relief in the battles we face, but let's not look too hard for a way out. Spring will come, but a "January thaw" is not always what we really need; it may come with hidden dangers. Persevere in the battle until the end. Jesus will strengthen you in every trial to the end of that test. He's promised to be with you.

"The Lord … will be with you. He will not fail you" (Deuteronomy 31:8).

The Search

THE HERFORD COW GRAZED nonchalantly on the side of a hill. I could tell by the size of her bag and her bloodied tail that she had a calf hidden in that vicinity. She occasionally looked down into the ravine, but other times she looked uphill. Her actions did not reveal where her newborn calf was hidden. It was a good ploy to throw me off.

We were gathering that pasture, and 280 pairs were bunched up near the gate, but this one cow had hidden her calf, and I knew that if I didn't find it, she might go quietly with the bunch. But leaving the cow behind to care for her hidden calf would cause extra work; someone would later have to bring in the pair. There was a chance that her calf was not yet born but was about to be.

I weighed the possibilities. If the calf was hidden and she went with the herd without fuss, she would surely be waiting at the gate the next morning to find her calf. But in the meantime, her calf could be discovered by predators, or should a storm move in, it could get hypothermia and weaken to the point of death.

I scoured the hillsides again, and this time I found it—a beautiful calf that had no interest in getting up and going until I brought his mother to arouse him and he wobbled after her.

Here's a lesson on finding valuable things in life: They don't always jump out at you. Sometimes we see evidence of where they might be and proof that things like peace and truth exist, but unless we patiently look for them, we will never find them. The best things in life don't just fall into our laps. We need to look for them, sometimes for years. Never give up seeking for the blessings that God wants to give you.

"Ask and you shall receive. Seek and you shall find. Knock and the door shall be opened unto you. For everyone who asks shall receive and he that seeks shall find and to him who knocks it shall be opened" (Matthew 7:7).

Lead Me

I‍T WAS M‍ONDAY MORNING, and the sun was right on the eastern horizon—a beautiful sight that a lot of people never see. A meadowlark was whistling out its greeting to a world that welcomed green grass and warm weather. We were briskly trotting our horses the mile and a half to the gate that led to the rock section. It had been a quiet ride so far, but when I dismounted to open the gate, I heard Slim ask the new hand—a heavyset, mustached cowboy with smooth chaps and large-roweled spurs—"What did you do yesterday?"

"I went to church," he replied with a grin. "My wife insisted, so I went, screaming and hollering all the way." We all laughed, picturing a little, petite woman leading a man his size in tears!

The idea of resisting something that is good for us was going through my mind as we sorted out pairs that we'd gathered that morning. We found a yearling in the bunch that obviously had crawled through the fence from the yearling pasture next to the rock section, where we'd gathered the 120 pairs we were working. Slim cut her out and took her to the gate, but she outmaneuvered him and rejoined the herd. The boss looked at me and said, "Put a rope on her and take her to the gate." I did, and despite her bellering and fussing, the heifer was finally where we planned her to be.

In our thoughts of spiritual life, we often resist God's tugging at our hearts to come and find spiritual life in Him. A visit to church might not be our idea of an enjoyable Sunday morning, but hearing about and eventually believing in Jesus Christ is a huge step toward eternal life, however much we resist it or hold back at the first leading.

"Search me, O God, and know my heart; try me and know my thoughts, and see if there be any wicked way in me and lead me in the way everlasting" (Psalm 139:23–24).

About the Author

ELDON TOEWS WAS BORN in Glasgow, Montana, in 1951 and grew up on his family's farm/ranch north of Frazer. He began to help with cattle work and breaking horses at a young age. By age thirteen, he was doing day work for neighbors, and at seventeen he went to work at the Ortman Ranch and later the Halverson Ranch.

Eldon attended Montana State University in Bozeman, during which time he spent the summers working on the Taylor Horse Ranch north of Fergus, Montana. In 1973, he graduated with a BS in animal science. He then spent a year working on ranches in Bolivia, South America. He returned to work on the Reno Creek Ranch and later Brooks Ranch near Crow Agency, Montana.

In 1976, Eldon married his childhood sweetheart, Carol Funk, and they began to work on a ranch in Washington State, during which time they spent some months in Israel, working on a cattle ranch on the Golan Heights. They returned to Montana in 1984 and helped on ranches near Busby and managed a ranch north of Red Lodge, Montana. They now live near Miles City, Montana, where Eldon helps on ranches while pastoring Living Way Fellowship church. They live on a small ranch east of Miles City and they have two sons, Quentin and Justin. These meditations were originally published in a weekly pastor's column in the *Miles City Star.*